STRANGER THAN FICTION

MONSTERS

Other **STRANGER THAN FICTION** *Books by*
Melvin Berger
From Avon Camelot

DINOSAURS
KILLER BUGS

Coming Soon
SEA MONSTERS

MELVIN BERGER is the author of over 100 books for young readers. He was born in New York City and has received degrees from the University of Rochester, Columbia University, and London University. He was elected to the New York Academy of Sciences in 1983.

His books have won many awards and honors and have been translated into 22 languages. Mr. Berger lives in Great Neck, New York, with his wife, Gilda, who is also an author of books for young people. The Bergers are the parents of two grown daughters.

MONSTERS

MELVIN BERGER

Illustrations by Kelly Oechsli

AN AVON CAMELOT BOOK

MONSTERS is an original publication of Avon Books. This work has never before appeared in book form.

AVON BOOKS
A division of
The Hearst Corporation
105 Madison Avenue
New York, New York 10016

Library of Congress Cataloging in Publication Data:
Berger, Melvin.
  Stranger than fiction : monsters / Melvin Berger : illustrations
by Kelly Oechsli.
    p.   cm.
  Summary: Describes monsters of the present such as crocodiles and vampire bats, monsters of the past such as dinosaurs and saber-toothed tigers, and two ''maybe monsters,'' the abominable snowman and bigfoot.
  1. Animals, Fossil—Juvenile literature.   2. Animals—Juvenile
literature.   3. Monsters—Juvenile literature.   [1. Animals.
2. Monsters.]   I. Oechsli, Kelly, ill.   II. Title.
QE765.B48   1991
597.6—dc20   90-45852

First Avon Camelot Printing: February 1991

CAMELOT TRADEMARK REG. U.S. PAT. OFF. AND IN OTHER COUNTRIES, MARCA REGISTRADA, HECHO EN U.S.A.

Printed in the U.S.A.

OPM 10   9   8   7   6   5   4   3   2   1

CONTENTS

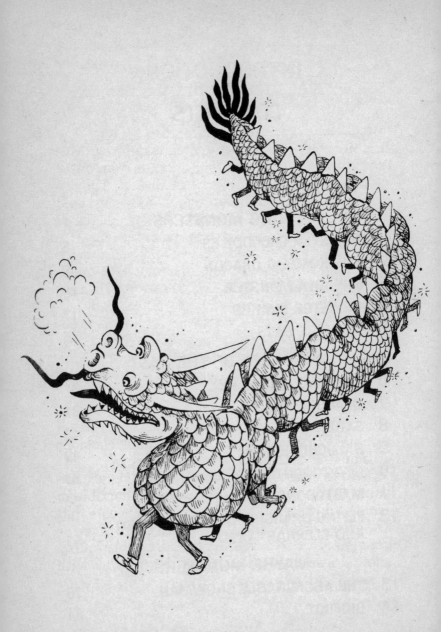

INTRODUCTION

Zombies, werewolves, dragons, vampires, Mutant Ninja Turtles, and scary beings from outer space are popular monsters of fiction. They're imaginary beasts invented by writers and moviemakers. They live only on the pages of books and on movie and television screens.

Amazing as they are, make-believe creatures don't compare to real-life monsters. Some monsters live on earth today. Others lived in ages past. But all are *stranger than fiction*.

Long ago, people called any unusual creature—human or animal—a monster. When they saw one, they expected terrible things to happen. The word itself originally came from the Latin *monstrum*, which means "to warn."

Today we understand our world much better. Most of us don't believe that monsters warn of trouble or signal disaster. And we don't consider all unusual creatures cause for alarm.

Still, monsters fascinate us. Monsters are animals that are strange, grotesque, or horrible in some striking way. They also include beasts that are exceptionally large, especially ferocious, or exceedingly loathsome. Just reading or thinking about these mysterious creatures fills us with wonder and awe.

Let's now enter the real world of monsters. We'll first take a close look at some spectacular monsters roaming the earth right now. They are among the most frightful animals of all time.

Next we'll turn to the most outstanding monsters from the past. Huge and fierce, some of these creatures once ruled the planet.

And finally we'll consider two mysterious "maybe" monsters. These puzzling creatures seem to live only in the most remote corners of our globe. Perhaps they exist. Perhaps they don't.

So read on. Meet a few incredible, honest-to-goodness, real monsters. See how they compare with the make-believe monsters of fiction and legend.

LIVING
MONSTERS

1
MONSTER CROCODILES

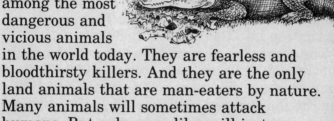

Crocodiles are
among the most
dangerous and
vicious animals
in the world today. They are fearless and
bloodthirsty killers. And they are the only
land animals that are man-eaters by nature.
Many animals will sometimes attack
humans. But only crocodiles will just as
soon kill and eat a human being as any other
animal.

An occurrence near the end of World War II
demonstrates how ferocious crocodiles can be.
On February 19, 1945, British troops had trapped about one thousand Japanese soldiers in an
island swamp near Burma.

All day long there had been heavy firing. The
Japanese were trying to break through the Brit-
ish lines. The British were trying to force the
Japanese to surrender.

Many crocodiles lived in the swamp. The
sound of gunfire sent them slithering into the
shallow water. During the day they floated qui-

etly in the water. Only their eyes and nostrils showed above the surface.

When darkness fell, the British stopped shooting and withdrew. Within moments, the crocodiles began to move. Silently they swam toward the groups of Japanese soldiers. Unable to escape in the soft mud, the soldiers watched helplessly as the monsters approached.

As soon as the crocodiles were within striking range, they attacked with savage fury. Stretching wide their huge jaws, the ferocious monsters lunged at their human victims. They dug their teeth deep into the soldiers' bodies.

The crocodiles' powerful jaws and teeth easily cut through uniforms, skin, bones, and flesh. But they were not able to rip off what they had bitten. So the enraged monsters flung their struggling captives about in the water. Sometimes they spun themselves completely around—jaws locked in place—to pull off the arm, leg, head, or chunk of flesh.

All night the bloodied waters churned. The swamp resounded with the noise of the frenzied crocodiles and the shrill screams of the Japanese. Around daybreak it grew very quiet. The British troops carefully entered the swamp.

What they saw horrified them. Only twenty Japanese had survived! A few had fallen victim to British gunfire. All the rest had been killed by the monster crocodiles!

Crocodiles are the largest and most deadly reptiles alive today. The ones found in the United States *(Crocodylus acutus)*, for example, are up to twenty-three feet long. Their weight can reach one thousand pounds.

Most crocodiles live in warm climates around the world. They are usually found on the shores of freshwater lakes, rivers, and swamps. These huge creatures are remarkably good, fast swimmers. Even though their hind legs are webbed, crocodiles don't paddle. They move ahead by wiggling their tails from side to side.

On land, the crocodiles slide about on their bellies. They can also walk on their legs with their bellies raised. When chasing their animal prey, they can gallop quite fast for a short distance.

Crocodiles spend most of the daytime hours sunning themselves on the shore. When they get too hot, they dip into the water or move under a shady tree. At night they feed in the water, usually near the shore. Turtles and fish are their favorite prey. So are birds and small land animals that are found in or near water.

Large crocodiles, though, often go after large game. Crocodiles in South Africa, for example, prey on antelopes, giraffes, buffalos, hippopotamuses, hyenas, wild dogs, porcupines, lions— and humans. In fact, the crocodiles in one South African national park killed more humans than all the other animals combined, including poisonous snakes!

Crocodile jaws are strong enough to bite through a thick wooden board. Yet if the jaws are shut, a human can easily hold them closed. The reason is that the crocodile has a set of powerful muscles to close its mouth. But the muscles to open the mouth are very weak.

The crocodile method of attack is eerie. First the crocodile grabs and holds its victim with its teeth. Then, since it feeds only in the water, it drags the animal into the lake, river, or swamp. The crocodile spins and twists and turns until it pulls a mouthful of flesh from the victim.

Holding the meat in its mouth, the crocodile lifts its head out of the water. With strange, jerky movements of its head, the crocodile knocks the meat down its throat. Bit by bit, it empties its mouth.

Sometimes a crocodile's teeth are not sharp enough to cut through an animal's thick skin. Then the monster uses a very clever trick to get its meal. It drags the animal's body down into the water. Here it wedges the dead animal between some rocks or fallen tree limbs. In time, the water softens the skin and starts to decay the flesh. Then the crocodile returns. It pulls the body out of the hiding place and devours it.

Many different types of crocodiles live around the world. Of all, the saltwater crocodile *(Crocodylus porosus)* is the most wicked and ruthless. This crocodile is a man-eating monster of the worst kind. An especially good swimmer, it is found mostly in the waters of southeast Asia and Australia. Although seldom longer than twenty feet, they can top the scales at an astounding two thousand pounds!

2

THE KOMODO DRAGON

The Komodo dragon (*Varanus komodoensis*) is a frightful, dangerous animal that looks like the dragon of myth and legend. True enough, this dragon doesn't breathe fire or swallow human beings whole. But the modern dragon does kill and eat animals as big as wild pigs, deer, and goats. And occasionally it does swallow humans—flesh, bones, and all.

According to scientists, the Komodo dragon is a lizard, the largest alive today. The biggest known specimen was taken to the St. Louis Zoo in 1937. It was ten feet two inches long and weighed 365 pounds. Average Komodo dragons are somewhat smaller—about eight feet long and two hundred pounds.

Komodo dragon is a good name for this monster, because it now lives only on the island of

Komodo and on some other small nearby islands. Komodo is part of Indonesia in Southeast Asia. The island is tiny—just twenty-two miles long and twelve miles wide.

The Komodo dragon was once much more widespread than now. But over the centuries, many were killed off by their natural enemies.

A number of dragons escaped death by swimming to Komodo. Even though the Komodo dragon is a land animal, it is a good, strong swimmer. Some have been known to swim as far as six hundred miles. The large animals that preyed on them were not able to follow them across the sea. So these Komodo dragons survived and lived on.

In time, though, humans settled on Komodo. They hunted the Komodo dragon for food. They captured them for zoos. Today there are no more than one thousand left in the world.

At first sight, the Komodo dragon looks like a powerful crocodile. Dull, dark, gray-black scales cover its slender body, big, broad head, and exceedingly long tail. Actually, the tail is as long as the entire body. It is so long that sometimes the dragon drags it on the ground. Other times, it holds it up in the air.

The Komodo dragon is a well-equipped killing machine. It has long, sharp claws on its paws. And its big, bright red mouth is lined with lots of small teeth. Each tooth is curved and as sharp as a knife, with a jagged, sawlike edge.

When hunting, the Komodo dragon rears up on its back legs. At the same time it utters a

The Komodo dragon's tail is as long as its body, as this photograph clearly shows

Negative No. 311791; courtesy Department of Library Services, American Museum of Natural History

low, weird hissing sound—*SSSSSSSSSS*. Its front legs dangle in the air as it swings its head back and forth, seeking a victim.

The Komodo dragon does not hear very well. But its good eyesight and keen sense of smell make up for this lack. Actually, the serpent uses its long, yellow, forked tongue to detect smells even at great distances. The tongue flicks in and out constantly, trying to pick up the odor of nearby animals.

Once it has picked up the scent, the cunning dragon darts off in that direction. Some say it can even outrun a fleeing deer!

The dragon catches its prey with its claws and teeth. Sometimes it puts its heavy tail to work as a battering club. Slashing, biting, and beating, the vicious animal quickly conquers its victims.

Having killed its prey, the Komodo dragon gets ready to feast. Holding the body in its claws, the dragon rips out huge chunks of meat with its sharp teeth. The animal stuffs much more food into its stomach than it really needs. When it can't force down another bite, the demon waddles off to its cave. There it sleeps for several days, digesting its immense meal. A Komodo dragon in a zoo once ate a whole deer. It then slept for a week!

3

THE GILA MONSTER

It's small—never longer than two feet.

It's ugly—with a fat head, small, beady eyes, brown, orange, and pink splotches on its body, and a short, stumpy tail.

And it's deadly—one-sixth of an ounce of its poison is enough to kill a man!

Despite its small size, this creature has earned the right to be called a monster—the Gila monster (pronounced HEE-lah; scientific name *Heloderma suspectum*).

The Gila monster lives in the dry desert lands of Arizona, New Mexico, and northern Mexico. It got its name because the first ones were found near the Gila River in Arizona.

During warm days on the desert, the Gila monster moves slowly and sluggishly. At these times it usually remains hidden under rocks or scrub bushes. But all through the cool nights, it prowls for food. The frightful beast can move very quickly after dark or when it's cold. But it never tries to catch fast-moving prey.

Any small or newborn animal makes a choice meal for a Gila monster. It also enjoys the eggs laid by birds or reptiles.

The Gila monster flicks out its long tongue to pick up the scent of a likely victim. A loud hiss is a signal that it has found its quarry. A sudden lunge—and the Gila monster has its teeth clamped into the animal's flesh.

But the monster's teeth are not sharp enough to cut through the meat. Instead it grinds and chews the flesh, working its teeth up and down until it can tear off a chunk.

As the Gila monster chews, its deadly poison, or venom, begins to flow. The venom comes from glands located in tiny sacs between the bottom lip and the lower teeth. The chewing motion forces more and more of the poison into the wound. The poison passes through grooves in the lower teeth. Within seconds, the powerful poison kills the Gila monster's victim.

Gila monsters very rarely attack humans. Mostly these beasts try to avoid human contact. They would much rather flee and hide. Also, Gila monsters can't move fast enough to catch any person who tries to run away. And they don't have teeth sharp enough to bite through shoes or heavy clothing.

Still, several people each year are bitten by Gila monsters. Curiously enough, most of the victims are drunk at the time. Others mistreat

The deadly Gila monster
Negative No. 310592; courtesy Department of Library Services, American Museum of Natural History

or tease the monsters. A few are careless in handling them in a zoo or laboratory.

The bites are poisonous. Sometimes they are fatal. Also, it is almost impossible to remove the Gila monster once it has sunk its teeth into a victim. Sometimes the beast must be pulled off with a pair of pliers. Human victims have been known to stagger into hospital emergency rooms with the animal still hanging from the wound!

Minutes after the bite, the venom starts to

15

work on the heart and respiratory system. The person feels weak and finds it hard to breathe. Vomiting, numbness, and a big drop in blood pressure may follow. The person loses consciousness and passes out. About one out of every four persons bitten by a Gila monster dies. Those who recover suffer pain and swelling from the bite for about ten days.

Since records have been kept, thirty-four Gila monster attacks on people have been reported. Twenty-six of these individuals survived. The other eight perished—victims of a modern killer monster!

4
MONSTER SNAKES

Most snakes are harmless. They do not bite or attack people. In fact, some are helpful. They eat animal pests that destroy crops. Other snakes, though, are extremely dangerous. Of the 2,400 different kinds of snakes, a few hundred are deadly to humans.

These killer snakes can be considered monsters if:

- their bite is poisonous to humans.
- they are large enough to squeeze someone to death.

In the United States, most poisonous snakes belong to the family of snakes known as vipers. Rattlesnakes, water moccasins, and copperheads are all vipers.

Most vipers have thick bodies and are not very long. Like many other kinds of snakes, vipers have heads that are broader than the rest of their bodies. Their eyes have catlike pupils.

In the viper's mouth are the venom, or poison, glands. That is where the snake makes and stores its poison. The venom is a clear, yellowish liquid that is made up of many different chemicals.

Snake venom is very powerful. The venom taken from just one viper is enough to kill eighty-four sheep. An even stronger venom, from the taipan snake, can kill two hundred adult men! Before there were drugs to fight the effects of taipan poison, only two men were ever known to survive its bite.

Ducts, or tubes, carry the poison from the glands to a pair of long, hollow teeth, or fangs, in the snake's upper jaw. When a poisonous snake, such as the rattlesnake, is about to strike, it opens its mouth extremely wide. The fangs point straight out. Then it slams its mouth shut on the victim. The two fangs pierce the skin.

Inside the fangs are hollow channels. The snake pumps venom through these channels and into the wound. It is like a doctor using a hypodermic needle to inject medicine into someone.

If the rattlesnake has caught a small animal or bird, the venom quickly kills. If the rattlesnake has bitten a human being, the person immediately feels the sharp, stinging pain of the bite. Then the venom starts circulating through the body.

Snake venom has two main effects. It attacks the central nervous system. This can paralyze the heart and the muscles necessary for breathing. And it attacks the red blood cells and the inner walls of the blood vessels. The result is internal bleeding.

The first symptom is swelling. The wound puffs up and the skin turns purple. After this, the victim becomes pale and sick to the stomach. The pulse beat grows weak and rapid. The person finds it harder and harder to breathe.

Some victims of snakebites recover by themselves. Others get to a doctor fast enough to have the wound treated. But in a number of cases, the bite is fatal. Of the one thousand Americans who are bitten by rattlesnakes every year, about twenty die.

Snakes catch and kill animals. But they cannot chew their prey. Their teeth are like long, thin needles. The teeth are wonderful for grasping, but they are of no use for breaking up large pieces of meat.

So the snake swallows its prey whole. Amazingly enough, a rattlesnake can swallow an animal up to three times its own size! Inside the snake's body, powerful juices in the stomach dissolve and digest the flesh of its victim.

All snakes are deaf. But they can feel vibrations through the ground. If someone shouts near a snake, the snake can't hear the sound. But if that person takes one light step, the snake senses the movement at once.

Snakes also have remarkable senses of sight and smell. But perhaps most astounding of all is their ability to detect heat. A rattlesnake can feel the heat from a mouse or other warm-blooded creature from up to six feet away!

Rattlesnakes are the best known and most feared of all poisonous snakes. They are found in every state of the United States, except Alaska and Hawaii and perhaps Maine and Delaware. Two types pose the greatest threat to humans: The eastern diamondback rattlesnake *(Crotalus adamanteus)* and the Texas, or western, rattlesnake *(Crotalus atrox)*.

The eastern diamondback is eight feet long and weighs thirty-five pounds. This snake is nasty and cranky. Unlike most other rattlers, it will sooner strike a person than slink away.

Far deadlier among American rattlers, though, is the western rattlesnake. This common snake has killed more people than any other kind of rattlesnake.

A rattlesnake can, of course, be recognized by its rattle. The sound is made by a set of horny rings loosely joined together at the end of its tail. The rattlesnake always lifts its tail when it shakes the rattle. No one knows its exact purpose. But experts guess that the rattle warns heavy animals not to step on the snake.

Rattlesnakes are known killers. But nearly 200 other kinds of snakes are just as deadly. Among the most feared is the coral snake, found in warm parts of the United States. Its broad red and black rings and narrow rings of light yellow make this snake pretty to look at. But the coral snake's bite is just as savage as that of the rattlesnake.

Indian snake charmers perform acts with another extremely poisonous snake, the cobra.

The rattlesnake shakes its rattle as a warning and to make its presence known

Negative No. 16391; photo by R.L. Ditmars, courtesy Department of Library Services, American Museum of Natural History

This venomous serpent, which lives only in Asia and Africa, seems to be swaying to the snake charmer's music. But the cobra, like all other snakes, is deaf. It is only following the side to side movements of the snake charmer.

Cobras poison their victims in two ways. Some bite them with their poison fangs. Others squirt, or spit, the poison at the eyes of the victim. In spitting, the cobra tilts back its head so that the poison shoots straight out.

Poison that lands on the skin causes no harm. But venom that gets into the eyes can lead to blindness if not washed out immediately. Far worse, though, is the bite. Bites can cause death in a matter of hours.

Many giant snakes don't have poisonous venom. They do, however, use their mouths to catch food. Their sharp teeth and powerful jaws are often enough to capture and kill their prey. Then, like the poisonous snakes, they swallow the victim in one big gulp.

When going after large game, though, a bite without poison doesn't always kill. The snake then wraps its huge body around the victim. Slowly it starts to squeeze.

The aim is not to crush or break the captive's bones. Rather, it is to suffocate, or stop the animal from breathing. Each time the victim breathes out, the snake tightens its grip a little. Meanwhile, the pressure makes it harder for the blood to circulate.

The lack of air and drop in blood flow hurt the creature. It passes out—and then dies. The snake relaxes its hold. Stretching its jaws wide open, the snake swallows the entire dead creature.

Snakes will eat almost any animal that they can get their jaws around. But because of their shape, they prefer long, thin animals, such as lizards or other snakes.

Monster snakes that kill by squeezing rarely attack human beings. But some people have died this way. The famed naturalist Roger Caras tells about a python that once crushed, killed, and swallowed a fourteen-year-old boy in Malaysia.

Pythons are among the biggest of the monster snakes. They are found in a few areas around the world. In India it's the Indian python *(Python molurus)*; in southeast Asia, the reticulated python *(Python reticulatus)*; and in Africa, the African rock python *(Python sebae)*. They are all dangerous beasts.

The pythons usually range in length from about twenty to thirty feet. A record 32-foot, 9½-inch reticulated python was shot in 1912 in Malaysia.

Pythons mostly eat small animals, no larger than a cat. But they have been known to eat creatures that weigh up to one hundred pounds.

The world's heaviest snake, the anaconda *(Eunectes murinus)*, lives in the hot, tropical parts of South America. An anaconda shot in Brazil in 1960 weighed a full five hundred pounds.

Anacondas are about as long as pythons, between twenty and thirty feet. But they weigh about twice as much as a python of the same length. Anacondas usually lurk on riverbanks, where they catch animals that come to drink.

Another type of big snake is the boa constrictor *(Constrictor constrictor)*. Some boas live in the southwestern parts of the United States. But most are found in tropical South America. At lengths between ten and eighteen feet, boa constrictors are smaller than other giant snakes.

Boa constrictors hunt while hanging from trees. When an animal—such as a rabbit or rat—passes underneath, the boa swoops down and bites. Then it winds itself around the stunned creature and squeezes until it dies.

Snakes are perhaps the most feared of all animals. In the case of the monster snakes, this fear is very easy to understand!

5

VAMPIRE BATS

The Spanish explorer Hernando Cortez lived during the sixteenth century. Like others of his time, he heard legends and folk tales about vampires. Vampires were said to be dead people who had risen from the grave. They were able to stay on earth as long as they drank the blood of living people.

Cortez landed on the coast of Mexico in 1519. The Indians there were terrified of a bloodsucking bat that lived among them. This ugly little monster drank human blood, just like the vampire of legend. So Cortez called the little monster "vampire bat." It was later given the scientific name *Desmodus rotundus*.

The habits of vampire bats are well known. During the day, they sleep. The bats hang, head down, in their homes—which may be caves, attics, or any other enclosed spaces. When it gets dark, the bats awaken. And they set out to find a meal of warm blood from a living creature—human or animal.

Sleeping humans are frequent targets. First

Vampire bat

the vampire bat hovers over the person like a miniature helicopter. If the person does not wake up, the bat lands nearby. Slowly and carefully it crawls to a patch of exposed skin. Its step is so light that the sleeper rarely awakens.

Very often the bat creeps to the sleeper's face. It seeks a place where the skin is thinnest and there are the fewest nerve endings. Earlobes and the tip of the nose are favorite spots.

Next, the little monster licks the area and nips it lightly with its teeth. If the victim stirs, the bat flits away. It waits awhile, and then tries another spot. Sometimes the bat will make several attempts before it finds a safe landing site.

Finally the vampire bat is ready to attack. It opens its mouth wide. This exposes its two long, razor-sharp canine teeth. Swish! The teeth slash down, slicing open the victim's skin. They cut so sharply and so quickly that most sleepers feel no pain.

Warm blood flows out of the two cuts. The vampire bat doesn't sip the blood so much as lap it up. It looks like a kitten lapping up milk from a saucer. The bat continues to drink the blood until it can't force down another drop. Sometimes it drinks its own weight in blood at one time. Then it flies away, sometimes with great difficulty because of the added weight.

Most victims lose too little blood to do any damage. They suffer few ill effects—unless, of course, the bat is carrying the virus that causes rabies. An infected bat can give the person rabies. If not treated, rabies is almost always fatal.

Vampire bats do not attack only humans. Very often they strike farm animals—cows, goats, and horses. Usually the bat zeroes in on a hairless, thin-skinned area. The back of the ear or the teats are favorites.

Some farmers take their livestock into the house at night rather than risk assaults by vampire bats. Many fear that the farm animals will become infected with rabies. Rabies drives animals mad. It causes them to go off on wild rampages, biting and destroying everything in their path.

Even vampire bats that are not infected can do animals lots of harm. Cows, goats, or horses bitten night after night lose a great deal of blood. In time they can grow weak and die.

Many different kinds of bats make their homes in the United States. But not vampire bats. Vampire bats are found only in Mexico and through Central and South America. Most of the human casualties of vampire bats have been reported from Brazil and Trinidad.

MONSTERS OF
THE PAST

6

TYRANNOSAURUS REX

Tyrannosaurus rex (tye-ran-uh-SAWR-us reks) was the biggest, most ferocious, and deadliest flesh-eating animal of all time. Its name means "tyrant king." This giant beast ruled all other dinosaurs on earth for millions of years.

Tyrannosaurus was well suited to its meat-eating way of life. Nearly twenty feet tall, the tyrant king stood as high as a two-story house. Exceptionally heavy, it weighed more than eight tons—one ton more than today's largest elephant. And fifty feet long, from the tip of its snout to the end of its long, heavy tail, it was twice the length of an army tank.

But of all aspects of *Tyrannosaurus*, its mouth was the most awesome. Set into its three-feet-long jaws were about sixty curved, six-inch-long teeth. Some teeth were as sharp as daggers, to cut through flesh. Others had jagged edges, to rip the flesh apart. When *Tyrannosaurus* slammed its huge mouth shut on a victim, the teeth slashed right through skin, flesh, and bone.

When attacking another dinosaur or other kind of beast, *Tyrannosaurus* opened its huge mouth a full three feet wide. A five-year-old child could stand upright between its gaping jaws. With a mouth this size, *Tyrannosaurus* took in more meat in one bite than an average man eats in a whole year!

This beast was also armed with other powerful weapons. On its back legs were sharp, eight-inch-long claws. *Tyrannosaurus* used these claws to attack and hold its prey before tearing out immense hunks of flesh with its teeth.

Until the middle of 1990, scientists thought that the dinosaur's short front limbs were of little use. But a *Tyrannosaurus* skeleton recently found in Montana showed that those limbs, too, were deadly weapons. At the end of these three-foot-long arms were claws that worked like meat hooks. The claws could dig deep into a victim's body and pick up weights as heavy as four hundred pounds.

A close study of *Tyrannosaurus* bones tells us that the monster walked slowly, probably around three miles an hour. It moved along the ground with its tail held straight out. The tail helped balance the dinosaur's heavy body. Even so, it waddled as it plodded along, lurching from side to side. Each small step made its

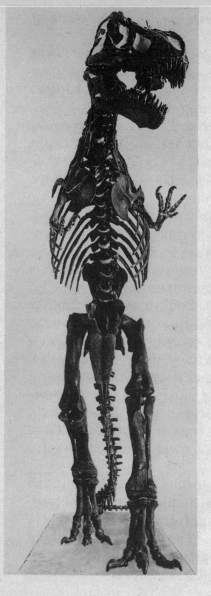

This frontal view of the skeleton of Tyrannosaurus rex shows the awesome set of teeth that earned the dinosaur its reputation as the fiercest flesh-eating creature of all time

Negative No. 5573; photo by A.E. Anderson, courtesy Department of Library Services, American Museum of Natural History

head bob back and forth, much like a chicken or pigeon.

At this speed, *Tyrannosaurus* could not have been a very good hunter. Most of its victims were probably animals too young or too old to flee, sick or injured, or already dead.

Most experts think that *Tyrannosaurus* could run fast for a short distance, so it could catch some active prey. Most likely *Tyrannosaurus* quietly hid in the bushes or trees. It waited there for its prey to come along.

As soon as *Tyrannosaurus* spotted its target, it bounded out. Jaws wide open, it flung its massive body against the startled animal. The power of the charge buried *Tyrannosaurus*'s long fangs deep in the unlucky creature.

The two beasts thrashed about in a mighty struggle. Blood spurted from the victim's deep wounds as it tried to escape *Tyrannosaurus*'s deadly grip. But each movement just dug the strong fangs deeper and deeper into its flesh.

In a little while, the battle was over. *Tyrannosaurus* had again proven itself king. It held the limp body with its rear or front limbs. Then it tore out big hunks of meat with its powerful jaws and teeth.

Finally the giant dinosaur had eaten as much as it could. Its skin was splattered with blood. Strips of raw flesh hung from between its teeth. Walking slowly now, *Tyrannosaurus* ambled away to digest its meal.

Tyrannosaurus lived from about seventy-one

million years ago until sixty-five million years ago. Most remains of this monstrous beast were found in what is now the western part of the United States and Canada.

7

BRACHIOSAURUS

Brachiosaurus (brak-ee-uh-SAWR-us) is by far the largest land animal that ever lived. It was super-super-big in every way:

Brachiosaurus measured eighty feet in length. If you put *Brachiosaurus* on a baseball field with its tail touching first base, its nose would almost reach second base.

At eighty tons, or 160,000 pounds, a single *Brachiosaurus* weighed as much as one thousand adult men.

Brachiosaurus could stretch up forty feet. If there had been buildings in those days, it could easily have looked into the fourth-floor windows.

Other measurements of *Brachiosaurus* were also immense:

- Its shoulders were twenty feet high—the height of a telephone pole.
- Its neck was thirty feet long—half as long as a bowling alley.
- A full-grown man would only reach up to the first joint of its front legs.

- The upper bone in its front leg was over seven feet long—taller than most professional basketball players.

The name *Brachiosaurus* means "arm lizard." It got that name for a good reason. It was the only plant-eating dinosaur whose front limbs, or arms, were longer than its rear limbs. The giant front limbs made the body slope downward from front to back. This shape is usually found only among meat-eating dinosaurs.

Brachiosaurus was stupendous in all ways but one. Its brain was ridiculously small. This huge monster had a brain about the size and weight of a hamburger bun!

In general, the bigger its brain, the more intelligent the animal. Thus, *Brachiosaurus* was far from smart. Most of what it did was guided by instinct, not thought.

Yet *Brachiosaurus* got along very well. One reason is that it was a plant eater. Surrounded by greenery, *Brachiosaurus* did not need to be very smart to find food. Neither did it need to be as clever or fast-moving as the meat eaters, who lived by hunting other animals.

Even the meat-eating dinosaurs were hardly a threat to *Brachiosaurus*. Its incredible size protected it from harm. The most ferocious dinosaurs could barely injure an animal the size of *Brachiosaurus*.

But *Brachiosaurus*'s tremendous size did create one problem. The monster was hungry all the time. It had to eat about a ton of food every day just to stay alive. Being a vegetarian made this less difficult than it could have been. Its diet of plants and leaves was always available. With little trouble it could reach branches beyond the reach of most other dinosaurs.

Some say that *Brachiosaurus* spent part of its time in swampy areas. If so, it most likely included water plants in its leafy diet.

One clue to *Brachiosaurus*'s eating habits is the shape of its teeth. Fossils show that they were shaped like chisels. Strong and sharp, they worked very well in pulling the leaves off trees and grinding them up.

Deep scratch marks and worn-down teeth give another clue to *Brachiosaurus*'s style of eating. The animal probably closed its mouth over a branch covered with leaves. Then it pulled its head back to strip the leaves off the branch. As it did, the hard branch scratched the dinosaur's teeth.

Most animals have their noses or nostrils at the front of their snout. Dogs and cats, horses and cows, goats and pigs, all do. But *Brachiosaurus* had its nostrils set in a ridge on the top of its head.

Why were the nostrils on top of the head?

For a long time, experts agreed that the position of the nostrils protected *Brachio-*

saurus. They guessed that when it sensed danger, *Brachiosaurus* waded into a nearby swamp, lake, or stream. It found a spot where it was completely underwater. Only its nostrils had to stick up above the water so that it could breathe.

This explanation seemed to make sense. But a few years ago scientists tested this theory. What they found surprised them. If *Brachiosaurus* stood in forty feet of water, the pressure of the water would collapse its lungs. It would not be able to breathe.

There has to be another explanation for the nostrils on top of the head. But thus far, none has been found.

Another puzzling feature of *Brachiosaurus*'s body was its very large nasal opening. Perhaps it gave *Brachiosaurus* a very keen sense of smell. Or maybe the big opening made the dinosaur's cries and calls louder and more booming. Possibly it helped *Brachiosaurus* to keep cool. The extra large surface of its nostrils may have rid its body of excess heat.

Many *Brachiosaurus* fossils have been found. This leads experts to believe that large numbers of these dinosaurs roamed the swamps and forests that covered the earth about 150 million years ago.

For the next 25 million years—until 125 million years ago—*Brachiosaurus* continued to thrive and multiply. But no remains have been found from later than 125 million years ago.

Their disappearance is another mystery.

Fossil remains of *Brachiosaurus* have been found on three continents—North America, Africa, and Europe. But many experts believe that these giant monsters lived all over the world.

8

SABER-TOOTHED TIGER

About twenty-five thousand years ago a mastodon, a huge, elephantlike creature, was lumbering across the flat plain in what is now southern California. The mastodon was heading for a shallow pool of water. The pool had formed in a patch of gooey black tar.

As the mastodon stepped onto the sticky black surface, its thick, heavy legs began to sink into the soft tar. The beast tried to pull its legs up. But they only slipped down, deeper and deeper. In a few minutes the mastodon was hopelessly trapped in the thick tar.

A large saber-toothed tiger (scientific name— *Smilodon*) was watching the mastodon from a clump of bushes. Seeing the mastodon stuck in the tar, the saber-toothed tiger came out of its hiding place. Fixing its bright, shining eyes on the mastodon, the saber-tooth slowly and carefully made its way forward.

The mastodon raised its short trunk and bellowed its helpless rage. But still the saber-toothed tiger advanced. When the saber-toothed tiger was a few feet from the mastodon, it stopped and crouched down low. Then, with a loud roar, it leaped forward.

The saber-tooth's long, sharp claws dug into the mastodon's thick, heavy neck. At the same time, the attacking beast flung open its huge jaws. They stretched so wide that its lower jaw touched its neck! Gleaming white in the bright sun were two fantastically long teeth curving down from the upper jaw. Each was about nine inches long. The edges were sharp and shaped like saw blades.

In an instant, the daggerlike teeth vanished. They sank deep into the mastodon's ample body with a snap of the saber-tooth's jaws.

The mastodon's blood spurted out, bright red, around the wound. The huge beast flung itself about, trying to shake off the cruel attack.

But the saber-toothed tiger held fast, its massive jaws locked in place. Struggle as it did, the mastodon could not rid itself of the attacker's death grip.

Finally the struggle was over. The mastodon was dead, held upright in place by the thick tar. The saber-toothed tiger released its tight hold.

But the pleasure of the kill did not last long. Slowly the saber-tooth, too, began to sink into the tar. It struggled in vain to pull itself out, but the tar claimed still another victim.

The saber-toothed tiger was named for the two dog teeth, or canines, on its upper jaw. Long, sharp, and pointed, they looked like curved

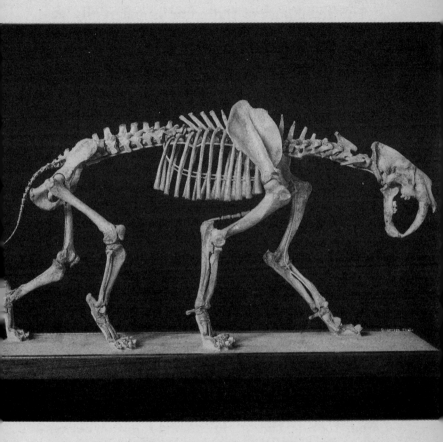

From this skeleton of a saber-toothed tiger, it's easy to see how the animal got its name

swords, or sabers. In the past, soldiers riding on horses used sabers to slash and stab their enemies.

The tiger part of the name is not really accurate. The saber-toothed tiger was not a tiger. It had longer, heavier front legs and shorter, weaker rear legs than the tigers of today. If anything, the saber-tooth looked more like a modern puma.

The saber-toothed tiger was up to 3½ feet tall at its shoulders. It weighed about six hundred pounds. Even though the saber-tooth had a small brain, we know that it was a successful hunter. It had a good sense of smell, which helped it find and track its prey. It had a strong, flexible body and powerful legs to launch its quick, savage attacks. And besides its saber teeth, it had back teeth that worked like scissors, cutting and slicing the meat it ate.

Since it was heavy and slow-footed, the saber-tooth never chased fast-moving animals. It much preferred sluggish mastodons, elephants, and rhinoceroses.

Saber-toothed tigers lived during the Ice Age, from about one hundred thousand years ago until perhaps twenty or thirty thousand years ago. Early humans lived at the same time as the saber-toothed tigers. But no one knows whether or not saber-tooths attacked humans.

Great numbers of saber-toothed tigers lived in Europe and America. About two thousand saber-toothed tiger skulls were found in the La

Brea Tar Pits of southern California alone.

Saber-toothed tigers were probably the most dreaded and most successful killers of that time. Yet saber-tooths died out at the end of the Ice Age. No one quite knows why.

9

BALUCHITHERIUM

In 1911 an English scientist, Sir Clive Forster Cooper, was digging for fossils in the area of modern Pakistan known as Baluchistan. In one dig he uncovered some amazingly big bones— three neck bones and a few foot and leg bones. He knew at once that they came from a giant monster. Cooper named the animal *Baluchitherium* (buh-loo-chuh-THIH-ree-um), meaning "Beast of Baluchistan."

In 1915 a Russian scientist named Borissiak discovered the remains of a similar immense animal. He was not aware of Cooper's discovery. But Borissiak had heard the Russian fairy tale about a huge monster named Indrik. Indrik could fly above the clouds. But when it walked on earth, every step made the earth shake and tremble.

Borissiak knew that Indrik was not real. But the bony remains reminded him of that make-believe beast. So he named the real monster *Indricotherium*, or "Indrik beast."

Some time later scientists concluded that *Ba-*

luchitherium and *Indricotherium* were really one and the same. Most call it *Baluchitherium*. Some, though, prefer to call it *Indricotherium*.

No matter whether it's called *Baluchitherium* or *Indricotherium*, the animal was stupendous.

Fact: *Baluchitherium* was thirty-seven feet long from nose to tail. That's longer than a full-sized school bus.

Fact: *Baluchitherium* was eighteen feet tall at its shoulders. That's as high as two school buses, one on top of the other.

Fact: *Baluchitherium* weighed thirty-three tons. That's equal to the weight of about twenty automobiles.

Fact: *Baluchitherium* could reach up twenty-five feet with its snout. That's nine feet higher than a giraffe can stretch.

Fact: *Baluchitherium*'s lower leg was five feet long. That's as tall as an average thirteen-year-old.

Fact: *Baluchitherium* had a narrow body that was supported by thick, heavy legs and wide, spongy, padlike feet. An adult man could not wrap his arms around one of *Baluchitherium*'s legs.

Although it was super-big, long-necked, and hornless, the *Baluchitherium* is closely related to today's rhinoceros. *Baluchitherium* did not need the protection of a horn because of its incredible size. What animal would want to start a fight with a thirty-seven-foot-long beast that weighed thirty-three tons?

Yet despite its great size, *Baluchitherium* was

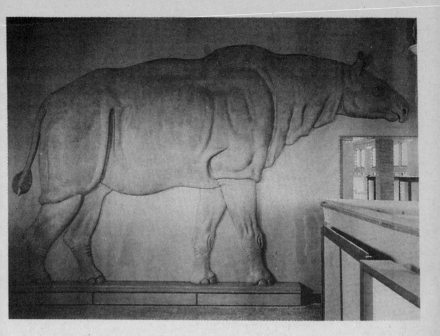

A model of Baluchitherium, the gentle monster closely related to the rhinoceros

Negative No. 314988; photo by C.H. Coles and Thane Bierwert, courtesy Department of Library Services, American Museum of Natural History

a gentle monster. It mostly ate the leaves growing high on trees. Its upper jaw had two thick, strong teeth to grab twigs and branches. And its upper lip came to a point to pull off the leaves.

Baluchitherium wandered in herds across the wooded plains of Asia between twenty and thirty million years ago. After that time, the forest land dried up and became a desert. And *Baluchitherium* died out—never to be seen again.

10

GLYPTODONTS AND ARMADILLOS

GLYPTODONTS

Among the most outlandish monsters from the past is *Glyptodont* (GLIP-tuh-dahnt). On the move, it looked like an armored truck slowly driving across a field. Fifteen feet long from snout to tail, five feet tall at its highest point, and weighing about four thousand pounds, the gigantic *Glyptodont* inched along like a big, heavy truck.

All animals, monsters and others, have enemies. And they need protection to fight off those that want to kill and eat them. Some have sharp claws and teeth. Others are very big, very strong, or very fast. Still others have keen senses that give them early warnings of danger.

But *Glyptodont* had its own special defense system. It consisted of a thick, solid, giant shell that covered the animal's body. The shell was made up of several tightly connected flat bones. Together they formed a single hard, bony shield.

Glyptodont skeleton, fully equipped with protective armor and clublike tail

Negative No. 35948; photo by A.E. Anderson, courtesy Department of Library Services, American Museum of Natural History

Glyptodont's bony armor even capped its head. And a series of bony rings protected its thick, heavy tail. The tail was tipped with *Glyptodont*'s only weapon of attack. It was a large knob covered with spikes sticking out in all directions. The knob resembled the mace clubs that knights carried long ago.

When *Glyptodont* was attacked by a flesh-eating animal, it could not run away. It was too slow and plodding in its movements. Instead, it would crouch down low, pull in its head, and bring down its shell.

In this position, the *Glyptodont* was safe. Its

enemy could find no opening to bite, stab, or slash. Only attackers that were smart enough to flip *Glyptodont* over on its back could do it any harm.

Driving away the attacker, though, was another matter. *Glyptodont* lashed out with its heavy, spiked tail. It swatted and whacked its enemy this way and that. Attacking animals that got too close were killed. At the very least, they were badly injured by the forceful blows and pointed spikes.

Glyptodont's favorite foods were the leaves and stems of green plants. But it also ate insects, worms, and the flesh of animals that were already dead. Its teeth were remarkably well suited to crushing and grinding leafy material. In fact, it was the raised rims and pattern of ridges on the flat tops of its teeth that led scientists to name the monster *Glyptodont*, which means "carved tooth."

The first *Glyptodont*s appeared on earth about two million years ago. These giants wandered freely over the pampas, the vast plains of South America. During the Ice Ages, some *Glyptodont*s migrated up to North America. All vanished, however, about ten thousand years ago.

Humans inhabited the earth the same time as the *Glyptodont*s. In fact, scientists have found a few human skeletons near *Glyptodont* fossils. Could early humans have used the monsters' huge shells as houses? Some think so. Others believe that the shells from smaller *Glyptodont*s served as coffins to bury the dead.

ARMADILLOS

*Glyptodont*s have been gone for many thousands of years. But a smaller animal that looks like *Glyptodont* can still be found today. This animal is called the armadillo, Spanish for "small armored one." The armadillos found in the United States are about two feet long and weigh up to fifteen pounds. They live from the southwest to the Atlantic coast.

The armadillo diet is much like that of *Glyptodont*. It includes plants, insects, worms, and the flesh of dead animals. In addition, armadillos also eat small snakes and frogs.

Like *Glyptodont*, the armadillo is covered by a shell of bony plates. But the plates are loosely connected with joints between the bands. When in danger, the armadillo can roll itself into a ball surrounded by its bony armor. The armadillo's shield also covers the top of its head, the outsides of its legs, and its tail.

When the armadillo senses danger, it can quickly dig a tunnel and hide underground. If it must fight, it uses the strong, sharp claws on its front legs to slash at the attacker.

Monster-sized armadillos can be found in Brazil. Some are nearly four feet long and weigh close to one hundred pounds. These hefty creatures are equipped with eight-inch claws on their front legs. Sometimes they use these claws to dig into fresh graves and pull out the flesh of corpses!

11

MASTODONS AND MAMMOTHS

MASTODONS

It was a clear day in January 1962. Two young boys, John Versace and Jimmy DiFranco, were walking across a field near their homes in Hackensack, New Jersey. Something half-buried in the ground caught their eye. It was big—about half the size of a football—solid, bumpy, and yellowish in color.

John and Jimmy dug around the object and freed it from the earth. Clearly it was a tooth. But its size was extraordinary. The tooth was hundreds of times larger than any human or animal tooth they had ever seen.

The youngsters had read about fossils and giant monsters from the past. They decided to wrap up the fossil and take it to a scientist.

The scientist recognized the tooth at once. It belonged to a huge, hairy, elephantlike monster called a mastodon (scientific name—*Paleomastodon*). The tooth the boys had found was between ten thousand and twenty thousand years old.

But mastodons had appeared in northern Africa long, long, before twenty thousand years ago. The first mastodon probably dates back about forty million years. It developed from an animal called *Moeritherium. Moeritherium* is the common ancestor of mastodons, mammoths, and modern elephants.

Moeritherium remains date back about sixty million years. *Moeritherium* was a small beast— no more than two or three feet tall. It was the size of a dog, between a cocker spaniel and collie in height. Its nose was big, and it had especially long incisor teeth on its upper and lower jaws.

Over the next twenty million years, *Moeritherium* grew much bigger. Finally it gave rise to the monster we call mastodon. Take the mastodon on exhibit in New York City's American Museum of Natural History. It is nearly ten feet tall at its shoulders and almost fifteen feet long. That's close to the size of an African bull elephant, the largest living descendant of *Moeritherium.*

Mastodons developed into perhaps one hundred different types. All had big, trunklike noses. The noses were long, though not nearly the length of the modern elephant's trunk. The mastodon could only reach up with its trunk. It could not swing it down.

Also, all mastodons had impressive tusks. The tusks were really very long incisor teeth growing from the beast's upper jaws. The tusks curved down toward the lower jaw. But they seldom grew to be more than six feet. Actually, six feet is long for a tooth, but short for a tusk.

The fearsome appearance of the mastodons also had to do with their exceedingly long lower jaws. Some jutted out over six feet. They were as long as the tusks.

The great tusks of *Ambelodon*, one type of mastodon, stuck straight out of its lower jaw. The two tusks were flat, like giant scoops and shovels. That's why these beasts are often called "shovel tuskers."

The massive *Ambelodon* lived on the shores of lakes. It probably used its flat tusks to scoop up immense quantities of the water plants it ate.

Most other mastodons lived in forest and woodland areas. The shape of their teeth—bumpy with many ridges—shows that they broke off growing plants and ground them up. In fact, one mastodon fossil was found with six bushels of twigs and chewed-up leaves in its stomach!

Early humans hunted mastodons during the Ice Age. They ate the meat. They made houses and tools from the bones and tusks. And they made clothes of the fur.

During the time mastodons lived on earth, between forty million and ten thousand years ago, they spread across Europe, Asia, and North and South America. In the United States, mastodon bones have been found all the way from New Jersey down to New Mexico.

The biggest single source of mastodon bones is the United States. More than one hundred mastodon skeletons have been dug up at a huge swamp known as Big Bone Lick in Kentucky.

MAMMOTHS

During the Ice Age, the fearful animal we call the woolly mammoth *(Mammuthus primigenius)* roamed widely in Europe and in North and South America. Its name came from the Russian word *mamot*, or "earth." Originally, people believed that mammoths lived under the ground.

The huge, hairy, elephantlike woolly mammoths had exceptionally long tusks. They were much longer than the tusks of today's elephants. The mammoth's tusks, like all tusks, never stopped growing. They first grew in a downward direction. Then they curved up and later began to head toward each other. This growth continued all the days of the animal's life. The longest mammoth tusks reached sixteen feet in length and weighed close to five hundred pounds.

Young mammoths used their short tusks for fighting and for digging up the roots of the plants, bushes, and trees that they ate. Older mammoths, with longer and more curved tusks, found them much harder to use. The animals seemed to use the long tusks mostly to clear away snow. This uncovered plants they could eat.

The woolly mammoth is the best known of these ancient monsters. Much of our knowledge comes from something that happened twenty-five thousand years ago on the bank of the Berezovka River in Siberia.

A woolly mammoth was making its way across the frozen, ice-covered land. Suddenly the huge beast stumbled. It let out a fearsome roar.

The heavy animal had stepped on a thin bridge of earth that had formed over a big crack in the icy glacier. Within seconds the monster plunged through the thin layer. It landed deep in the crack.

The animal was badly hurt by the fall. Its hip and leg bones and some ribs were smashed. The beast struggled to escape its icy prison. But it was too firmly wedged in the ice to get out. After a few hours it died and became frozen rock-hard.

Layers of ice and soil soon formed on top. For many thousands of years the frozen body lay there. It remained in one place, untouched by germs or animals of prey.

Then, gradually, the climate grew warmer. The ice melted. Rain and landslides washed away the layers over the frozen body and exposed it to the air. Germs caused the beast to decay. Animals tore out pieces of its flesh.

Soon the carcass began to rot. In August 1900 a peasant and his dog were out hunting reindeer. The dog picked up the stench of the rotting remains and led his master to the spot.

The peasant ignored the body parts that lay half-buried in the ground. But he was thrilled to see one giant tusk. He knew that such tusks were worth lots of money.

The man took the tusk back to his village and sold it to a trader. Delighted with his payment, the peasant quickly forgot about the body in the ground.

Fortunately, the trader reported the finding to the Academy of Sciences. After a year or so, the Academy sent a scientific expedition to the site where the tusk had been found. What they discovered astounded them: It was the nearly perfectly preserved body of a woolly mammoth that had died twenty-five thousand years earlier! Almost all of its bones, flesh, skin, hair—even the food in its stomach from the last meal—were there, and in very good condition.

From the Siberian mammoth and other quick-frozen fossils, scientists have formed a complete picture of these gargantuan monsters. Their shaggy appearance came from a dark red-brown coat of hairs, up to twenty inches long. Under the hairs was a one-inch layer of soft, yellowish wool. And beneath the wool and skin was a 3½-inch layer of fat. The fat helped them survive the freezing arctic temperatures.

The stomach contents of the Siberian mammoth weighed twenty-eight pounds. It included fir cones, pine needles, flowers, and moss. The monster probably had to keep eating all the time to keep up its weight—which was around ten thousand pounds.

The woolly mammoth was roughly twelve feet tall at its shoulders. But there was another mammoth, the imperial mammoth (Mammuthus imperator), that was even bigger. It had a shoulder height of fifteen feet.

The imperial mammoth was found to the south of the woolly mammoth. Since it lived in warmer climates, it was probably not covered with fur or long hair.

Early cavemen hunted both types of mammoths with spears. But the spears had to be very

A model of the imperial mammoth

sharp and flung with great strength to pierce the thick mammoth skin.

The hunters also had another way to capture these mammoths. They dug big pits in the ground. And they covered the holes with branches and leaves. When mammoths walked over the branches, they fell into the pits. Hunters then killed the animals by bombarding them with heavy rocks.

The mammoths disappeared between ten thousand and eight thousand years ago. Changing conditions on earth were the probable cause. The warmer weather and melting ice at the end of the Ice Age doomed the woolly titans. The imperial mammoths died out later. Changing climate and growing numbers of people destroyed the forests that were home to these mighty monsters.

12

FLYING DRAGONS, GREAT TERRORS, AND ELEPHANT BIRDS

FLYING DRAGONS

The "Flying Dragon," or *Pteranodon* (tair-AN-uh-don), lived at the time of the dinosaurs, from about 150 million years ago to perhaps 65 million years ago. It was not a dinosaur. But it was an extremely odd-looking flying monster.

The *Pteranodon* body was about the size of a very big turkey. It measured four feet long and weighed about thirty pounds. But its wings stretched out a remarkable twenty-seven feet, the wingspan of some fighter jets!

Each wing consisted of a thin web of skin. It extended from the exceedingly long fingers on the front limbs to the sides of the body. Added to this bizarre arrangement were three other fingers at the front of each wing. Each front limb, then, was equipped with both wings *and* claws!

Perhaps even more striking was *Pteranodon*'s

oversized head. Most of the head was taken up with its three-foot-long toothless, pointed beak.

The Flying Dragon's grotesque appearance was topped by a long, raised bony crest. The crest ran from the sharp tip of its beak back beyond its head. The end looked like a lengthy, straight horn.

Typically, the Flying Dragon sat high on a cliff over the water. Its clever eyes glistened in the sunlight as it stared down. Suddenly it spread its amazingly wide wings and lifted off its perch. Down it swooped, hardly flapping its wings at all. Skimming above the surface, it tossed its bony-crested head back and forth. Each turn sent the birdlike monster off in a new direction, zigzagging over the salty sea.

Suddenly the ugly beast plunged its two legs into the water. In a flash its powerful claws grabbed a silvery gray fish darting about near the surface.

A few flaps of its immense wings then carried the *Pteranodon* to a rising current of air. The monster gently floated up to its perch. Folding its wings, it settled down to devour its struggling prey.

Pteranodon was not a bird. It had wings, but no feathers, and every bird has feathers. Actually, *Pteranodon* was a reptile, like snakes, lizards, and turtles.

Even though *Pteranodon* could fly, it could not fly very well. It was more of a glider, using its wings to float on currents of air.

Many *Pteranodon* fossils have been found in

the present state of Kansas. *Pteranodon* lived there when that area was covered with a vast sea. Its ample brain and oversized eyes made it well equipped for catching fast-moving fish and other swift, but small, marine animals.

GREAT TERRORS

Pteranodon's disappearance from earth about sixty-five million years ago was followed by the arrival of an even more monstrous flying creature. Nicknamed "Great Terror," it has the scientific name *Diatryma* (die-uh-TRY-ma). Most fossils of *Diatryma* have been found in what is now New Mexico and Wyoming.

Pteranodon was a reptile—but it could fly. Great Terror was a bird—but it could not fly. It had feathers and wings, but its wings were too small to pull its huge body up into the air. Standing about eight feet tall, it was a foot or so taller than any player in today's National Basketball Association!

Great Terror looked more like a small version of the monstrous *Tyrannosaurus rex* than a bird. But unlike the heavy-footed dinosaur, Great Terror was a strong, swift runner. Some say it was fast enough to prey on ancestors of the horse that lived at the same time.

ELEPHANT BIRDS

The "Elephant Bird," or *Aepyornis maximus* (ee-pee-OR-nis MAX-ee-mus), is a far more recent monster. It lived until just over one hundred years ago. People who saw this extraordinary creature described it in books and letters. They say it stood about ten feet high and probably weighed close to one thousand pounds.

Like the Great Terror, the Elephant Bird had wings but couldn't fly. Built like an ostrich, it had a tiny head at the end of its long neck. Most striking were its legs, which were as thick as tree trunks.

The Elephant Bird was first mentioned in a book written by the French admiral Étienne de Flacourt, in 1658. He spotted the monster on the island of Madagascar off the east coast of Africa. (Madagascar is now called Malagasy Republic.)

Over the following two hundred years, many other Elephant Birds were spotted—but only on Madagascar. The last positive sighting of the Elephant Bird was in 1867. But some say a few others may still be hidden in remote spots on the island.

Why did the Elephant Bird live only on one island in the world?

Very likely, none of its natural enemies lived on the island. With no animals to threaten this gigantic creature, it could grow and multiply without limit. In fact, a similar bird, *Dinornis maximus*, also existed only on one island in New Zealand.

Why, then, did it disappear? As humans settled on Madagascar, they cut down thousands

71

of acres of forest land. This left less room for the Elephant Bird. It also led to less rainfall and the drying up of the remaining forests. With the disappearance of the swampy forests came the extinction of the Elephant Bird.

Humans contributed to the extinction of the Elephant Bird in another way. The early settlers looked on this huge, heavy monster as a wonderful source of food. Hunting the Elephant Bird also reduced their numbers.

The Elephant Bird has a unique claim to fame. Its eggs are the very largest eggs of any bird—living or dead. One of its eggs in the British Museum is about fifteen inches long and twelve inches across. It weighs twenty-seven pounds and holds over two gallons of liquid!

MAYBE
MONSTERS

13

THE ABOMINABLE SNOWMAN

The history of the Abominable Snowman reaches back about twenty-five hundred years. Information on this baffling monster has been collected, bit by bit, over all this time. Today the bits make a rather convincing picture of a real-life monster—part human, part ape.

The "Wildman," *ye ren* in Chinese, was first mentioned in writings in China, around 500 B.C. Wildman was described as six feet tall with human features, but completely covered with hair. His image appeared in a number of ancient drawings and paintings. His picture was even printed on some very old currency.

British army officer L. A. Waddell, in his 1899 book *Among the Himalayas*, told of finding phenomenal footprints on a snowy trail high in the Himalayas. These are the mountains that separate India from Tibet and China. The native guides recognized the prints at once. They told Waddell the prints were made by large, hairy wild men who lived in the snow-capped regions.

Two decades passed. Lieutenant Colonel C. K.

Howard-Bury of the British army led an expedition to Mount Everest in the Himalayas. At a height of about twenty-one thousand feet, the men noticed a far distant, dark figure making its way across the snow. They tried to track him down. They found a trail of gigantic footprints where he had been seen. The snowy imprints were human in shape—except that they were three times the size!

Some Tibetans on the expedition were terrified. They said the prints belonged to *Metoh Kangmi*, or "Abominable Snowman." Others called it *Yeti*, which means "Magical Creature."

Each Tibetan gave a slightly different impression of the monster. But all agreed that the creature was heavy, apelike, around six feet tall, and very hairy. Its humanlike face had white skin, and its mouth revealed very long teeth.

They also said that the Abominable Snowman had long, powerful arms that hung down to its knees. The strong, agile creature could bound across the mountains at high speeds. And it could hurl immense rocks as though they were pebbles.

The next believable sighting of an Abominable Snowman came in 1925. British photographer, naturalist, and fellow of the Royal Geographical Society N. A. Tombazi was also trekking in the Himalayas. At a height of fifteen thousand feet, Tombazi saw the monster. It stood no more than two or three hundred yards away. Until then, the scientist had doubted the existence of the Abominable Snowman. But for him, seeing was believing.

Captain d'Auvergne, curator of India's Victoria Memorial, was the next eyewitness. He was climbing alone in the Himalayas in 1938 when he became blinded by the snow and fell ill from exposure. When d'Auvergne returned home, he told how a nine-foot Abominable Snowman carried him to a cave, fed him, and nursed him back to health.

In 1951 two British mountaineers, Eric Shipton and Michael Ward, climbed a glacier twenty thousand feet up in the Himalayas. There they found and photographed footprints that were eighteen inches long and thirteen inches wide. Whoever made them was big and heavy, walked on two feet, and had only four toes on each foot. Later, an article in the British medical journal *The Lancet* concluded that the prints might have been made by an unknown monster.

More information continued to pour in.

In 1954 a London newspaper sent an expedition to the Himalayas to search for the Abominable Snowman. They didn't find the monster. But they came back with a few hairs from a three-hundred-year-old scalp kept in a Buddhist temple. The scalp was monstrous—eight inches high and twenty-six inches around. The hairs were sent to a laboratory. The scientists said the hairs came from no animal known at present.

A. G. Pronin, a professor of science at Leningrad University in Russia, spotted an Abominable Snowman in 1958. The professor was scouting in the Pamir Mountains of Central Asia. At first glance, he took it to be a bear. But then he realized that it was a manlike creature.

It was walking on two feet, upright, but in a stooping fashion. It was naked, and its thickset body was covered with reddish hair. The arms were overlong and swung with each movement. He watched it for about ten minutes before it disappeared, very swiftly, among the scrub and boulders.

A mountain-climbing team from England in 1979 also sighted the Abominable Snowman in the Himalayas. They heard the monster's loud screams. And they found footprints—eight inches long and four inches wide—that showed four toes and a thumb. Each print pressed the snow down about three or four inches—a sign that the creature walked upright and weighed about 160 pounds.

Team members followed the tracks. They found that the Abominable Snowman had jumped down from some rocks, run across the snow, and then walked onto an outcrop of stone. At that point they lost the trail.

The accounts of the Abominable Snowman and similar monsters start and end in China. In 1990 scientists collected some hairs believed to have been left on trees, bushes, and the ground by Wildman. They studied these hairs under a scanning electron microscope at a university in China. The conclusion? The hair structure was unlike that of any other animal known to humans.

Some of the hairs were taken to another university. Here they were analyzed chemically in an advanced particle accelerator. The hair was found to contain chemicals like those in both humans and apes. But the exact makeup was not like either species.

Abominable Snowman. Yeti. Wildman.

Are these different names for one kind of real, live monster?

Why have there been so few sightings and contacts through history?

Does this monster live only in remote parts of the world?

Or are the man-apes rarely seen only because there are so few of them?

These are very tough questions to answer. Some experts believe the facts add up to proof that the monster does exist. Others say that only the capture—dead or alive—of one of the creatures will be proof positive.

And for now, that's where the matter stands.

14

BIGFOOT

The northwest corner of the United States and the southwest corner of Canada in North America are very far from the Himalayas in Asia. Yet this area is home to a monster that may be related to the Abominable Snowman.

This North American monster is usually called Bigfoot. It got this name simply because its tracks are so long and wide. In Canada it is also called Sasquatch, an Indian word meaning "hairy giant."

Bigfoot looks much like the Abominable Snowman. It stands between seven and nine feet tall and weighs approximately six hundred to nine hundred pounds. Built like an ape, it is covered with hair, walks upright, and has arms that seem too long for its body. Its footprints are about sixteen inches long and six inches wide.

Bigfoot lives in the thick mountain forests of northern California, Oregon, and Washington. It has also been spotted in the southern part of the Canadian province of British Columbia. Humans find it hard to get around in these areas.

Yet there have been more sightings of Bigfoot than of the Abominable Snowman. And a number of reliable witnesses have described actual encounters with Bigfoot.

The most convincing meeting occurred on June 10, 1982. Paul Freeman of the United States Forest Service was strolling along an old logging road in the Blue Mountains near Walla Walla, Washington. To his shock and amazement, an "enormous creature" suddenly stepped out into the road from between some bushes.

The creature was only about two hundred feet away. Freeman could see it very clearly. He said the figure was eight feet tall and walked on two legs. Its arms dangled to its knees, and its body was covered with reddish brown hair. Freeman also reported that the beast gave off an awful stench.

For an instant, Freeman and the monster stared at each other. "I've never been so scared in the woods before," he later wrote. "This thing was real. It was big enough to tear the head right off your shoulders."

Fearing for his life, Freeman turned and fled. As he ran, Freeman looked back. He was relieved to see the creature also running—but in the opposite direction.

Freeman hurried back to Forest Service Headquarters. He told the others of his face-to-face meeting with Bigfoot. A group headed back to the old logging road. They didn't see the beast. But they did find a trail of twenty-one huge, human-shaped footprints.

Phil Thompson and his partner found this footprint, 17 inches long and 7 inches wide, while hunting in Oregon. Is this proof of the existence of Bigfoot?

Photo courtesy UPI/Bettmann

Each print was fourteen inches long and seven inches wide. Though they were on hard ground, each one had sunk down an inch or more. This proved that the monster was very heavy. Art Snow, an expert in tracking, followed the trail for three-quarters of a mile. But then he lost it.

Freeman's sighting was quite recent. It reminded people of an important early encounter. This one took place on July 3, 1884, near the town of Yale, British Columbia.

Engineer Ned Austin was at the controls of a train heading to Yale when he saw what looked like a man asleep at the side of the tracks. He stopped the train.

The noise awakened the man, who jumped up and started to run away. Austin now saw that the creature was manlike, but not human. Since the train was ahead of schedule, the crew decided to give chase.

The men soon caught the beast, tied him up, and brought him back to the train. The crew named him Jacko and placed him in the baggage car. Then the train went on to Yale.

When they arrived, everyone inspected Jacko closely. He was small—only four feet seven inches tall and 127 pounds. His build and features were human. But his body was covered with inch-long dark, glossy hair.

Jacko's arms, though, were not like human arms. They were much longer. And much more powerful. He could easily break a stick that most men could barely bend.

When Jacko spoke, he barked or growled. And

he seemed to prefer a diet of fresh milk and berries.

The railroad crew left Jacko in Yale. The story is hard to follow after that. Some say the town put him on exhibit. Another rumor says that he was sold to a circus.

President Theodore Roosevelt, in his 1893 book *The Wilderness Hunter*, told of the dangerous side of Bigfoot. Roosevelt wrote that an experienced woodsman, identified only as Bauman, went hunting with a partner in the mountains in Oregon. After setting up camp, they left to scout the area.

They returned at dusk to find the camp destroyed. Their packs were ripped open and the contents scattered about. The lean-to was smashed.

Certain that the attacker was a bear, the men set up the camp again. Only then did Bauman's partner take a close look at the tracks. "Bauman," he called out, "that bear has been walking on two legs."

Deeply troubled, the two men went to sleep. At midnight, Bauman was awakened by some noise and a strong smell. He made out a giant figure in the darkness. Quickly grabbing his rifle, he fired at the shape. But he missed. A loud rustling in the underbrush made him think some big, heavy creature was fleeing into the woods.

The men were gone until dusk the next day setting out their animal traps. When they got back, they found the camp was torn apart a second time. This time they checked the tracks very carefully. Sure enough, it appeared that a big, two-footed monster had caused all the trouble.

Neither man could sleep that night. At about midnight they again heard—and saw—something very startling. By moonlight they could see a monster standing poised for nearly an hour on a hillside overlooking the camp. From time to time it uttered a harsh, grating, moanlike sound. But it made no move toward the camp.

Although experienced and armed, Bauman and his partner were scared. They made up their minds to leave the woods the very next day.

At sunup, they started to collect their traps. By the end of the day, they had gathered all but three. Bauman suggested that his partner go back, break camp, and pack while he collected the remaining traps.

The sun was setting when Bauman returned. His partner had packed all of their belongings. But the man was nowhere to be seen. Bauman looked everywhere. Then he saw him, stretched out on the ground. He was dead. The man's neck was broken and four bloody slash marks crossed his throat.

Leaving everything behind, Bauman grasped his rifle and fled. He ran and ran until he reached the meadow where the two men had left their horses. He leapt on his mount and rode away as fast as he could.

Finally, an especially strange and bizarre event in the history of Bigfoot—or in this case, Sasquatch—came to light in 1957. That year,

Albert Ostman told of the incredible adventure he had some thirty-three years earlier.

Ostman was out prospecting in the mountains near the coast of British Columbia. On his third night in the wilderness, he was asleep in his sleeping bag. Suddenly he felt himself being picked up, sleeping bag and all, and carried for some distance.

Ostman tried to wriggle out of the sleeping bag. But he was too tightly wedged in to move. For three hours Ostman was carried in the arms of a big, strong, unseen creature. Then he was roughly dumped on the ground.

Ostman crawled out and saw four hulking monsters hovering over him in the dark. They appeared to be a man, a woman, and two children. The man was about eight feet tall, stocky, long-armed, and covered with hair. The others had the same build, but were somewhat shorter and slimmer. All had sloping foreheads and rather pointed heads.

Ostman had been kidnapped by a family of Sasquatches! For six days they fed and cared for him. But every time he tried to escape, one of them blocked his way. On the seventh day, though, he managed to free himself. Only the female tried to stop him. But Ostman scared her by firing his rifle over her head and he got away.

Ostman ran all day and slept in the woods that night. The next day he heard the sound of a distant engine. He followed the sound and came upon a logging camp. After resting up for a few days, he headed back to civilization.

For thirty-three years Ostman kept his story to himself. He was sure that no one would believe him. Then, as more and more stories about Bigfoot and Sasquatch came out, he decided to give his account.

Biologist John Napier read the details. He stated that everything Ostman said could be true. Magistrate A. M. Naismith, a former criminal lawyer, cross-examined Ostman and tried to break his story. He, too, decided that Ostman was telling the truth.

Is this proof that Bigfoot is an actual, living monster? No one is sure.

Only one thing is certain. True monsters—and maybe monsters—are fascinating creatures. What's more amazing than...

- today's vicious man-eating crocodiles and scary vampire bats?
- the huge, ferocious *Tyrannosaurus rex* and deadly saber-toothed tigers of long ago?
- the mysterious half man/half ape monsters found only in remote mountain areas?

Real monsters *are* indeed stranger than fiction!

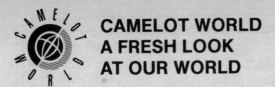

CAMELOT WORLD
A FRESH LOOK
AT OUR WORLD

THE MYSTERIOUS CAT
76038-X/$2.95 US/$3.50 Can

by Elizabeth Garrick

People have lived with cats for nearly four thousand years, yet they still remain a mystery. This book will tell you everything you want to know about cats, like why they purr and why they always fall on their feet.

HOT MACHINES
76039-8/$2.95 US/$3.50 Can

by Gregory Pope

Learn about the fastest, coolest, meanest vehicles on earth. From 1,400-miles-per-hour fighter jets to 200-miles-per-hour racecars, this book will take you on a tour of the most exciting land, sea, and air vehicles in the world.

SECRETS OF THE SAMURAI
76040-1/$2.95 US/$3.50 Can

by Carol Gaskin

For nearly 900 years, the best fighters in the world dominated the island of Japan. These were the samurai and the ninja, who terrorized their enemies with bow and arrow, spear and sword.

A KID'S GUIDE TO HOW TO SAVE THE PLANET
76041-X/$2.95 US/$3.50 Can

by Billy Goodman

In the last few decades, your home planet has been overwhelmed by a host of environmental problems like oil spills, acid rain, toxic waste, and the greenhouse effect. Read this book and find out how you can help.

Sixty-two tricks you **can** do!

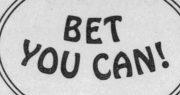

Science Possibilities to Fool You
by Vicki Cobb and Kathy Darling
illus. by Stella Ormai

Make a sugar cube float. Pour light. Hold water in a sieve. Keep a friend in a chair with just one finger. Bet you can! This amazing collection of challenges that seem impossible—but aren't—will delight and entertain while teaching about the human body, matter, energy, and other scientific principles.

Avon Camelot Original

82180-X • $2.95 US/$3.50 CAN

Also by Vicki Cobb and Kathy Darling
BET YOU CAN'T! *Science Impossibilities to Fool You*
54502-0 • **$2.95** U.S. $3.50 CAN.